POLAR BEARS

POLAR BEARS

Mark Newman

Henry Holt and Company
New York

ACKNOWLEDGMENTS

Special thanks to Ivy Stone for suggesting that I create a children's book on polar bears, and for introducing me to her book agent friend, Carolyn French, who in a stunningly short time sold the idea to Henry Holt Books for Young Readers. Also thanks to the following: the friendly folks at Henry Holt—Eve Adler, Sally Doherty, Laura Godwin, Véronique Sweet—for their enthusiasm, creativity, and suggestions; my good friend, Sammye Seawell, founder and director emeritus of the Alaska Zoo, for access to Ahpun, a four-month-old polar bear orphan; and Mike Sieve and Matt Breiter, for accompanying me on various trips to Churchill, Manitoba.

Henry Holt and Company, LLC, *Publishers since 1866*
175 Fifth Avenue, New York, New York 10010 [www.HenryHoltKids.com]

Henry Holt® is a registered trademark of Henry Holt and Company, LLC.
Copyright © 2011 by Mark Newman
All rights reserved.
Distributed in Canada by H. B. Fenn and Company Ltd.

Library of Congress Cataloging-in-Publication Data
Newman, Mark.
Polar bears / by Mark Newman. — 1st ed.
p.   cm.
ISBN 978-0-8050-8999-8
1. Polar bear—Juvenile literature. I. Title.
QL737.C27N49 2010   599.786—dc22   2009029416

First Edition—2011 / Designed by Véronique Lefèvre Sweet
Printed in July 2010 in China by Macmillan Production Asia Ltd.,
Kwun Tong, Kowloon, Hong Kong (Supplier Code 10), on acid-free paper. ∞

10 9 8 7 6 5 4 3 2 1

To my mother and father, Estelle and Harry

Polar bears are big.

The polar bear is the biggest
bear in the world. They're even
bigger than the Kodiak brown
bear. A giant male polar bear
can weigh 1,700 pounds—that's
about as heavy as a small car.
Females usually weigh less than
males. One polar bear was said
to weigh 2,200 pounds. That's
more than a ton of bear!

Polar bears are tiny.

Polar bears weigh only one pound at birth. They will grow to thirty times their birth weight by the time they leave the den. A mother polar bear is not able to eat while she nurses her babies from January to April. By then mother polar bears are very hungry!

Polar bears are twins.

Most polar bear mothers
give birth to twins. Although
polar bears usually do not
hibernate, expectant mother
polar bears do. Mating
occurs in mid-spring and
females dig a den into a
snowdrift in the fall. Babies
are born inside the den in
early January. The den is
cozy, staying 40 degrees
warmer than the frigid
Arctic air outside.

Polar bears struggle.

Baby polar bears will stay with their mother for over two years
as she teaches them all the skills they will need to make it into
adulthood. But being a baby bear is not easy. Three out of four
do not survive to see their third birthday.

PACIFIC OCEAN

NORTH AMERICA

ALASKA

NORTH POLE

ASIA

CANADA

ARCTIC OCEAN

RUSSIA

U.S.A.

GREENLAND

NORWAY

EUROPE

ATLANTIC OCEAN

AFRICA

Polar bears live only in the north. Unlike penguins, they do not live in the Antarctic. Penguins and polar bears never get to meet in the wild. Polar bears live in only five countries, all of which surround the North Pole: Russia, Canada, the United States (Alaska), Norway, and Greenland.

Polar bears live in the Arctic.

Polar bears are not really white.

Despite what they look like and what most people think, polar bears are black, not white. Under all that warm thick fur their skin is totally dark. The fur itself is made up of clear hollow hairs, sort of like hollow tubes, that contain no color whatsoever. The bears look like they are white only because their clear hair reflects light.

Polar bears are patient.

Polar bears are very patient hunters. Their main diet is the ringed seal, which is the most numerous seal in the Arctic. They can smell a seal's breathing hole in the ice. Then they wait silently until the seal surfaces at that particular hole. This can take a very long time, since each seal has ten or even fifteen different holes to choose from. Sooner or later the seal returns and the giant bear grabs him.

Polar bears are hungry.

Polar bears like to eat only the blubber and skin of the seal and usually leave the meat, which is in turn scavenged by arctic foxes. A bear can eat 100 pounds of seal fat at a single sitting. Polar bears need to catch about one seal a week in order to stay strong and healthy. When the opportunity presents itself, which is rarely, polar bears will even hunt walruses and beluga whales.

Polar bears are tough.

Polar bears are masters when it comes to enduring blizzards and cold weather. They have lots of warm fur, even on the bottoms of their feet. But equally important is their four-inch layer of blubber. With this combination of fur and blubber almost no heat escapes from their body, even when the arctic temperature drops to minus 50 degrees Fahrenheit. A polar bear's body temperature stays at a steady 98.6 degrees, the same as ours. Their compact ears and very short tail further prevent heat loss.

Polar bears are fast.

No other four-legged animal can swim as fast as the polar
bear. They swim at a rate of six miles per hour. That's
quite a bit faster than they generally walk. They can do
this because of their dinner-plate-size front paws, which
are webbed and work like paddles. They use their hind
legs only to steer. Their great swimming ability gives
them their Latin name, *Ursus maritimus*, which
means "sea bear." They are also good divers
and can see well underwater.

Polar bears are few.

Altogether there are only 20,000 to 25,000 polar bears in the world. These are separated into 19 groupings, which are called subpopulations. Most polar bears, about 15,000, live in Canadian territory. About 4,000 live in northern Alaska in two separate groups. There are no polar bears in the middle or southern part of Alaska.

Polar bears are endangered.

For tens of thousands of years polar bears were the undisputed rulers of the far north. But now their existence is in jeopardy. Climate change is their single greatest threat. When the sea ice breaks up and melts earlier and earlier each spring, the bears find it increasingly difficult or impossible to catch seals. The result has been that in certain regions fewer baby bears are surviving since their mothers are not as well nourished. Pollution and the disturbance caused by northern oil rigs and exploration for oil are additional threats. The United States Department of the Interior declared the polar bear a threatened species— the first animal added to the endangered species list because of global warming.

MORE FACTS ABOUT POLAR BEARS

Of the eight species of bears in the world, the polar bear is the most recent, having evolved from the brown bear just 200,000 years ago. It is ironic that this most recent bear may become the first to disappear.

Although the polar bear population today is currently healthy, its future is in grave peril due to global warming. One-third of all polar bears may be gone in the next 45 years as the Arctic ice melts at an ever-increasing rate. Hudson Bay's subpopulation of polar bears has already experienced a 22 percent decline, from 1,200 bears in the 1980s to only 935 today.

In Canada and Russia, more polar bears are seen on land—where they don't belong—as the ocean's ice shrinks. This is causing conflict with humans. In 2006, some 180 bears came ashore around the remote Siberian town of Vankarem (pop. 140), necessitating that patrols be organized to protect the villagers. In March 2008, a juvenile polar bear wandered inland more than 250 miles to the Alaskan village of Fort Yukon. No one in the village could remember having ever seen a polar bear in the area. In early April

2008, three polar bears walked 240 miles south from the Arctic coast to Deline in Canada's Northwest Territories. They had no body fat and were starving.

Polar bears that have not resorted to coming ashore have to swim ever greater distances between ice floes. They can easily swim 15 or even 30 miles with no problem. But when that distance becomes 50 or more miles, especially when the seas are stormy, they are at risk of becoming exhausted and sometimes drowning. Four were observed drowned in 2004.

In August 2008, nine polar bears were spotted swimming way off Alaska's northwest coast. Their fates are unknown.

In May 2008, the United States Department of the Interior listed the polar bear as *threatened* under the Endangered Species Act. Also, the International Union for Conservation of Nature (IUCN) has added the polar bear to its Red List. This is a start. If we want future generations to be able to experience the thrill of knowing that the polar bear is still alive and well and roaming the far north, we must take actions now that

will reverse the effects of climate change on the habitat of this Arctic icon.

The following is a list of conservation organizations concerned with the future welfare of the polar bear:

- **Bear Conservation Fund**
  15542 County Road 72
  Warba, MN 55793
  www.bearbiology.com

- **Center for Biological Diversity**
  P.O. Box 710
  Tucson, AZ 85702
  www.biologicaldiversity.org

- **Defenders of Wildlife**
  1130 17th Street, NW
  Washington, DC 20036
  www.defenders.org

- **International Fund
  for Animal Welfare**
  290 Summer Street
  Yarmouth Port, MA 02675
  www.ifaw.org

- **IUCN/International Union
  for Conservation of Nature**
  Rue Mauverney 28
  1196 Gland
  Switzerland
  www.iucn.org

- **National Wildlife Federation**
  11100 Wildlife Center Drive
  Reston, VA 20190
  www.nwf.org

- **Natural Resources Defense Council**
  40 West 20th Street
  New York, NY 10011
  www.nrdc.org

- **Polar Bears International**
  105 Morris Street, Suite 188
  Sebastopol, CA 95472
  www.polarbearsinternational.org

- **World Wildlife Fund**
  1250 Twenty-fourth Street, NW
  P.O. Box 97180
  Washington, DC 20090
  www.wwf.org

SOURCES INCLUDE:

- Barringer, Felicity. "Polar Bear Is Made a Protected Species." *New York Times*, May 15, 2008. www.nytimes.com/2008/05/15/us/15polar.html.
- *CBC News*. "Wandering Polar Bears a Sign of Climate Change: Expert," April 3, 2008. www.cbc.ca/canada/north/story/2008/04/03/deline-bears.html.
- IUCN Polar Bear Specialist Group. "Unprecedented Loss of Sea Ice Renews Concerns for Survival of the World's Polar Bears," Polar bear status report. *Polar Bears International*. July 6, 2009. www.polarbearsinternational.org/polar-bear-status-report.
- Mahan, Tammy L. "Evolution of the Polar Bear." *Helium.com*. n.d. www.helium.com/items/374037-evolution-of-the-polar-bear.

AUTHOR'S NOTE

I have always loved all forms of wildlife and over the past 30 years have traveled to the seven continents to observe and photograph many different species. As you would expect, polar bear photography involves dealing with some of the harshest weather anywhere. Most of my polar bear images were shot during late fall trips to Churchill, Manitoba, on the western shore of Hudson Bay, a region known as the polar bear capital of the world. Hundreds of bears congregate along the shoreline, waiting for the ice to freeze so they can head out to hunt seals.

On my first polar bear trip, a friend and I simply rented a pickup truck and drove around the frozen tundra looking for bears. This was not the most efficient way to get photographs but it was certainly exciting. One polar bear came around the passenger side of the pickup and pounded on the window with his paws. We had to drive away quickly. Another climbed into the back of the truck as we watched from a safe distance. Temperatures fell below minus 50 degrees Fahrenheit with wind chill. Warm clothing was as important as good camera gear. I never

could keep my fingers warm and they often became so numb that I couldn't feel the shutter release button.

On a subsequent visit, I went the traditional route and utilized the safe and comfortable tundra buggy from which to take pictures. These vehicles are half again as tall as a standing bear and move around the tundra on huge oversized tires. Not as exciting as a pickup truck, but much more practical for quality photography.

There were certain pictures I could not obtain in the wild, so I turned to various zoos for help. I'm not a diver and I don't even like cold water. Fortunately for me some zoos have modern polar bear exhibits with large pools allowing for underwater observation. The bears don't play in the water all day, but after repeated visits to multiple zoos I was able to obtain some excellent underwater imagery.

And then there was Ahpun, an orphaned female polar bear cub who was rescued and brought for care to the zoo in my hometown of Anchorage, Alaska. She was barely four months old and weighed only 31 pounds when she arrived. She needed around-the-clock attention but the small zoo didn't have enough professional staff for this at the time. So volunteers watched the little bear during the daytime. I spent several memorable days as a volunteer keeper, playing with the cub and at the same time taking advantage of the photo opportunity.

I hope you enjoy seeing these photos as much as I enjoyed taking them.